LET'S TALK ABOUT IT

"A GUIDE ON HOW TO BE A GREAT FRIEND"

"A COMPREHENSIVE GUIDE ON BUILDING AND NURTURING MEANINGFUL CONNECTIONS"

BY

P. A. MALONE

Let's Talk About It

"A Guide on How to Be a Great Friend"

"A Comprehensive Guide on Building and Nurturing Meaningful Connections"

By

P. A. Malone

Copyright © 2024 by P. A. Malone

All rights reserved. No part of this book may be reproduced.

Dedications:

"To my dearest sister Toni and my cherished best friend Chalonda.

In the tapestry of friendship, you two have woven the most vibrant threads into the fabric of my life. This book is a celebration of the extraordinary bond that connects us, and it wouldn't be complete without acknowledging the profound impact you've had on my journey.

Toni, your unwavering support, infectious laughter, and the countless shared secrets have filled my life with joy. Your friendship is a testament to the enduring strength of family bonds, and I am grateful every day to have you by my side.

Chalonda, my confidante and partner in crime, your friendship has been a guiding light on both the sunniest days and the stormiest nights. Your loyalty, empathy, and the countless adventures we've embarked upon are the essence of true friendship, and I am fortunate to call you my best friend.

This book is dedicated to both of you, who have exemplified the essence of being great friends. May these pages inspire others to cultivate the kind of bonds we share—a friendship that withstands the test of time, triumphs over challenges, and brings immeasurable joy.

With All My Love,

P.A. Malone

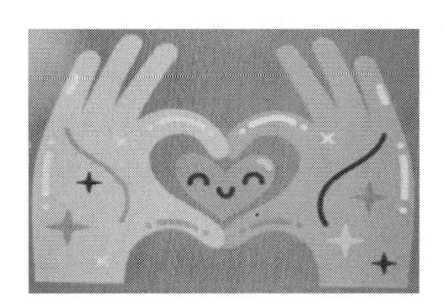

Preface:

Embracing the Art of Friendship

In the tapestry of life, woven with the threads of experience and connection, there exists a masterpiece called friendship. It is a profound relationship that transcends time and circumstance, shaping the contours of our existence with laughter, shared moments, and a tapestry of emotions. This book aims to explore the art of being a good friend, a craft that requires a delicate balance of understanding, empathy, and unwavering support.

As we navigate the intricate landscapes of our lives, the role of a true friend becomes a guiding compass, pointing us toward authenticity, companionship, and shared growth. In these pages, we will delve into the fundamental principles that form the foundation of meaningful friendships, discovering the traces that transform acquaintances into confidantes and mere connections into bonds that withstand the test of time.

From the enthusiastic highs of joyous celebrations to the somber lows of challenging moments, the essence of a good friend remains a constant presence. Through the narratives and reflections within this book, we embark on a journey that celebrates the beauty of friendship, explores the details of communication, and unveils the secrets to cultivating lasting connections.

In a world often marked by humanity, the ability to be a good friend is a timeless virtue. It is an art that transcends cultural boundaries, defies the limitations of distance, and flourishes in the fertile soil of mutual respect and understanding. As we embark on this exploration of friendship, let us open our hearts to the lessons within, discovering how the simple yet profound act of being a good friend can transform our lives and the lives of those we hold dear.

So, let the journey begin—a journey into the heart of friendship, where the brushstrokes of kindness, loyalty, and compassion come together to create a masterpiece that is as unique and enduring as each of us.

Welcome to the exploration of the art of being a good friend.

The Heart of Friendships - Active Listening

Unlocking Connection:

Discover the essential role of active listening in friendships. This chapter explains why being a good listener is crucial for building strong connections. Understand how active listening influences trust and understanding in all kinds of friendships.

Simple Listening Tips:

Learn easy yet powerful tips to become a better listener. From eye contact to paraphrasing, these practical techniques empower you to engage more in conversations and strengthen your bonds with friends.

Fun Listening Exercises: Practice and refine your listening skills with hands-on exercises. These fun and interactive activities are designed for real-life situations. By the end of the chapter, you'll not only grasp the importance of active listening but also have practical tools to use in your friendships.

Examples:

Scenario: A friend is going through a tough time at work. Active listening involves expressing empathy and providing comfort.

Tip: Maintain open body language and nod occasionally to show you're engaged.

Exercise: Role-play a conversation where you actively listen to a friend's problem.

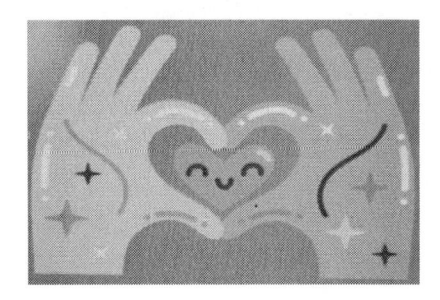

Supportive Friendships Through Thick and Thin

Being There Always:

Explore the importance of being a reliable friend in good and challenging times. This chapter looks at the essence of companionship during both joy and sorrow. It applies to everyone, from teens to the young at heart.

Celebrate Together:

Discover creative ways to celebrate each other's victories, big or small. This is a vital aspect of any friendship. The chapter includes ideas for joyful shared moments that contribute to a supportive and uplifting friendship.

Comfort and Empathy:

Learn how to provide genuine support during tough times. Explore the role of empathy in strengthening the bond between friends facing challenges. This advice is relevant for friends of all ages.

Examples:

Scenario: Your friend is celebrating a promotion. Being there involves sharing joy and acknowledging their success.

Tip: Send a thoughtful congratulatory message or plan a small surprise celebration.

Exercise: Reflect on a challenging situation where you provided comfort to a friend.

Embracing Differences in Friendships

Friendship Mosaic:

Friendships are enriched by unique qualities. This chapter emphasizes the beauty of diversity and how celebrating individuality creates a vibrant connection. It's a universal message for everyone.

Navigating Disagreements:

Learn practical strategies for handling differing opinions with grace and respect. This is a natural part of any relationship. The chapter teaches you how to foster healthy and resilient friendships.

Strength in Diversity:

Explore how embracing differences enhances the depth of a friendship. This is a strength that applies to friends of all ages, broadening perspectives and fostering personal growth.

Examples:

Scenario: You and your friend have different political views. Navigating this involves respecting differences and finding common ground.

Tip: Focus on understanding their perspective before expressing your own.

Exercise: Engage in a friendly discussion about a topic you disagree on.

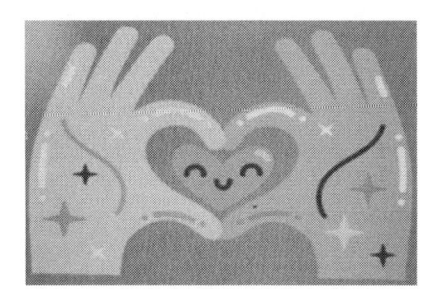

Building Trust in Friendships

Timeless Trust:

Trust is the cornerstone of lasting friendships. Understand how to build and maintain trust over time. This chapter explores the key components that create a trustworthy foundation, relevant to people of all ages.

Reliable Reputation:

Being seen as reliable is crucial for fostering trust. Practical tips guide you in establishing a reputation that instills confidence in your friends. Actions that build trust are discussed, and applicable to friendships across generations.

Navigating Trust Issues:

Trust can be fragile. This chapter offers guidance on addressing breaches with sensitivity and resilience. It explores the process of rebuilding relationships after trust has been compromised, emphasizing open communication and commitment.

Examples:

Scenario: Your friend shared a personal secret. Building trust involves keeping that confidence.

Tip: Be consistent in your actions and follow through on promises.

Exercise: Discuss a situation where trust was tested and how you navigated it.

Open Communication for Stronger Bonds

Creating Openness:

Open communication is vital for healthy friendships. Discover the importance of creating an environment where friends feel comfortable expressing themselves. The chapter discusses vulnerability and authenticity in fostering open and honest communication for all ages.

Expressing Effectively:

Effective communication involves more than just speaking. Learn to express thoughts and feelings in a way that ensures understanding. Practical tips and examples guide you in articulating your emotions and thoughts, contributing to deeper connections with friends.

Overcoming Communication Challenges:

Communication challenges can be overcome with the right approach. This chapter addresses common pitfalls and provides strategies for clear and constructive communication, applicable to friends of all ages.

Examples:

Scenario: Misunderstandings arise due to lack of communication. Open communication involves addressing concerns promptly.

Tip: Use "I" statements to express feelings without blaming.

Exercise: Practice expressing your feelings on a sensitive topic with a friend.

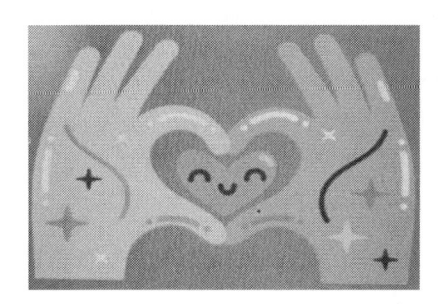

Understanding and Empathy Across Lifetimes

Recognizing Struggles:

Empathy is explored as the bridge connecting hearts in friendships. Understand the importance of recognizing and validating each other's struggles across all ages. Explore how understanding the emotional landscape of friends contributes to supportive and compassionate connections.

Cultivating Empathy:

Empathy is a skill that can be cultivated at any age. Practical exercises guide you in developing empathetic abilities. Explore the life-changing power of empathy in strengthening the bonds of friendship.

Building a Supportive Foundation:

A foundation of understanding is crucial for lasting friendships. This chapter discusses how empathy and mutual understanding create a supportive environment. By embracing empathy, you'll foster deeper and more meaningful connections with friends, applicable to all ages.

Examples:

Scenario: Your friend is going through a challenging time. Empathy involves acknowledging their feelings and offering support.

Tip: Listen without judgment and validate their emotions.

Exercise: Practice active listening in a conversation about a friend's struggles.

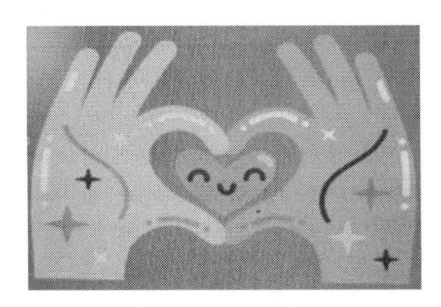

Gratitude and Appreciation

Expressing Gratitude for Your Friend's Presence:

Gratitude is a powerful force in friendships. This chapter explores the importance of expressing gratitude for the presence of your friends in your life. We'll discuss the positive impact of acknowledging the value your friends bring to your journey.

Simple Gestures to Show Appreciation:

Appreciation is often conveyed through small, thoughtful gestures. Practical ideas and examples will inspire you to express your gratitude in meaningful ways. From handwritten notes to acts of kindness, these gestures contribute to a positive and appreciative mindset.

A Positive and Thankful Mindset: Fostering a positive and thankful mindset enhances the quality of friendships. We'll explore the life-changing effects of cultivating gratitude in your daily interactions. By the end of this chapter, you'll understand how a thankful outlook contributes to a fulfilling and joyous friendship.

Examples:

Scenario: Your friend helped you through a tough time. Expressing gratitude involves acknowledging their support.

Tip: Write a heartfelt thank-you note or plan a small gesture of appreciation.

Exercise: Reflect on a friend's impact on your life and express your gratitude to them.

Reliability in Friendship

Being a Dependable Friend:

Reliability is a cornerstone of trust in friendships. This chapter delves into the importance of being a dependable friend – someone others can rely on in various situations. We'll explore practical ways to demonstrate reliability and build a reputation as a trustworthy companion.

Providing Practical Assistance

Being there for your friends goes beyond emotional support. This section discusses the role of practical assistance in solidifying the bonds of friendship. From lending a helping hand to offering practical advice, we'll explore ways to be a reliable and supportive friend.

Strengthening Bonds Through Reliability

Reliability contributes to the strength of friendships. We'll discuss how consistent and dependable actions strengthen bonds with friends over time. By embodying reliability, you'll contribute to the resilience and depth of your friendships.

Examples:

Scenario: Your friend needs help moving. Being reliable involves showing up on time and helping.

Tip: Offer specific ways you can help and follow through on commitments.

Exercise: Recall a situation where your reliability made a positive impact on a friend.

Example:

Your friend consistently follows through on promises and commitments, making them someone you can rely on.

Scenario:

Your friend promises to help you with a DIY project over the weekend.

Tip: Acknowledge their reliability and strengthen the bond by expressing your appreciation. In the future, reciprocate by being just as dependable, reinforcing trust and reliability in your friendship.

Apology and Forgiveness

The Importance of Sincere Apologies:

In any friendship, conflicts and misunderstandings are inevitable. This chapter emphasizes the significance of offering sincere apologies when needed. We'll explore the elements of a genuine apology and discuss how it contributes to the resolution of conflicts.

Learning to Forgive and Let Go:

Forgiveness is a crucial aspect of maintaining healthy friendships. We'll discuss the life-changing power of forgiveness and how it liberates both the forgiver and the forgiven. Practical insights will guide you in cultivating a forgiving mindset in your friendships.

Rebuilding Trust After Conflicts:

Conflicts can strain trust, but it's possible to rebuild. This section provides a road map for rebuilding trust after conflicts. From open communication to consistent actions, we'll explore the steps to fostering renewed trust in your friendships.

Examples:

Scenario: You unintentionally hurt your friend's feelings. Offering a sincere apology involves acknowledging your mistake.

Tip: Apologize without excuses and show genuine remorse.

Exercise: Reflect on a situation where forgiveness played a key role in preserving a friendship.

Example: You inadvertently forgot about a dinner date with your friend, causing disappointment.

Scenario: Your friend expresses their feelings of being let down after you missed the dinner date.

Tip or Solution: Apologize sincerely, acknowledge their feelings, and make amends by planning a special outing to demonstrate your commitment to the friendship.

Learn from the mistake and make a conscious effort to be more considerate of plans in the future.

Celebrating Together

Acknowledging and Commemorating Milestones:

Celebrating milestones is an integral part of friendship. In this chapter, we'll explore the significance of acknowledging and commemorating important events in your friends' lives. We'll discuss creative ways to celebrate together, strengthening the bonds of camaraderie.

Planning and Organizing Special Celebrations:

Creating memorable celebrations requires thoughtful planning. Practical tips and ideas will guide you in organizing special events for your friends. Whether it's a birthday, an achievement, or a spontaneous gathering, we'll explore ways to make these moments special.

Creating Lasting Memories in Friendship:

Shared celebrations contribute to the tapestry of lasting memories in friendships. We'll discuss the importance of creating meaningful and lasting memories with your friends. By the end of this chapter, you'll be inspired to cultivate a culture of celebration, enhancing the joy and longevity of your friendships.

Example:

Your friend just got a promotion at work, a significant milestone worth celebrating.

Scenario: Organize a surprise party with close friends to acknowledge and commemorate your friend's achievement.

Tip: Personalize the celebration by incorporating elements that reflect your friend's interests. It could be a themed party, a dinner at their favorite restaurant, or even a weekend getaway. The key is to make the celebration meaningful and tailored to their preferences.

Respecting Personal Boundaries

Understanding the Importance of Personal Space:

Respecting personal boundaries is essential for maintaining healthy friendships. This chapter explores the concept of personal space and why it's crucial for the well-being of individuals in a friendship. We'll discuss the role of understanding and respecting each other's need for space.

Setting and Respecting Boundaries in Friendships:

Healthy friendships thrive on mutual respect for boundaries. Practical insights and examples will guide you in setting and respecting boundaries in your friendships. We'll explore how clear communication and understanding contribute to a harmonious balance in relationships.

Navigating Differences in Comfort Levels:

Individuals have varying comfort levels in friendships. This section addresses the importance of navigating these differences with sensitivity and respect. By understanding and adapting to each other's comfort zones, you'll foster an environment of trust and acceptance in your friendships.

Examples:

Scenario: Your friend needs space after a challenging experience. Respecting boundaries involves giving them time and space.

Tip: Communicate openly about boundaries and be receptive to your friend's needs.

Exercise: Share experiences where respecting personal boundaries strengthened your friendships.

Example:

Your friend values personal space, especially after a busy week.

Scenario:

Your friend communicates that they need some time alone over the weekend.

Tip or Solution: Respect their need for solitude by sending a supportive text, expressing understanding of their need for personal space. Avoid excessive communication during this time, allowing them the peace they seek.

Encouraging Growth in Each Other

Supporting Personal and Professional Aspirations

True friends encourage each other to pursue their dreams. In this chapter, we'll explore the role of supporting personal and professional aspirations in friendships. We'll discuss how being a cheerleader for your friends contributes to a culture of growth and fulfillment.

Motivating and Cheering on Your Friend's Goals

Motivation is a powerful force in achieving goals. Practical tips and insights will guide you in motivating and cheering on your friends as they pursue their aspirations. By being an active supporter, you'll contribute to the success and happiness of your friends.

Growing Together in a Friendship

Friendships, like individuals, are meant to grow. This section discusses the concept of growing together in a friendship. We'll explore how shared experiences, mutual support, and continuous communication contribute to the ongoing development of meaningful and lasting connections.

Examples:

Scenario: Your friend decides to start a new business. Supporting their aspirations involves offering encouragement and practical help.

Tip: Be genuinely interested in your friend's goals and provide constructive feedback.

Exercise: Reflect on a situation where your encouragement positively impacted your friend's growth.

Nurturing Long-Distance Friendships

Embracing the Distance:

Explore the challenges and opportunities that come with maintaining friendships across geographical distances. This chapter delves into the importance of adapting to different time zones, schedules, and communication methods to keep the connection strong.

Virtual Bonding Activities:

Discover creative ways to stay connected with friends who are far away. This chapter provides a variety of virtual bonding activities, from online gaming to virtual movie nights, to help bridge the physical gap and create shared experiences.

Overcoming Communication Barriers:

Communication can be challenging when miles apart. Learn effective strategies to overcome communication barriers, including the use of technology and setting regular check-ins. This chapter aims to empower you to maintain meaningful connections regardless of the distance.

Examples:

Scenario: Your friend has moved to another country for work. Nurturing the friendship involves finding new ways to connect and understanding their adjusted schedule.

Tip: Schedule virtual coffee dates or plan periodic video calls to catch up.

Exercise: Share experiences where adapting to distance strengthened your friendship.

Example:

Your childhood friend has moved to a different time zone for a job opportunity.

Scenario:

Coordinate a virtual game night that accommodates both time zones, allowing you to enjoy shared activities despite the distance.

Tip & Solution:

Choose games that can be played online or consider asynchronous options, such as turn-based games, to make it easier to connect. This way, you maintain a sense of togetherness and create lasting memories, despite the physical separation.

Weathering Changes in Friendships

Friendship Evolution:

Friendships, like any other aspect of life, change. This chapter explores the natural evolution of friendships and how individuals and dynamics can change over time. Understanding these shifts is crucial for maintaining resilient and adaptable connections.

Adapting to Life Transitions:

Life transitions, such as marriage, parenthood, or career changes, can impact friendships. Learn how to adapt and support friends through various life stages. This chapter provides insights into maintaining connections despite evolving circumstances.

Rekindling Old Friendships:

Friendships from the past may fade, but they can also be reignited. This section offers guidance on rekindling old friendships, including practical steps to reconnect and rebuild meaningful bonds.

Example:

Your friend is starting a family and has less time for socializing.

Scenario:

Plan virtual meetups that accommodate their schedule, such as a weekend afternoon video call.

Tip & Solution:

Acknowledge the changes in their life and express understanding. By trying to stay connected in ways that align with their new responsibilities, you show your support and maintain the friendship.

The Role of Laughter in Friendships

The Power of Laughter:

Laughter is a universal language that strengthens bonds. This chapter explores the importance of humor in friendships, from light-hearted jokes to shared funny experiences. Discover how laughter contributes to joy, resilience, and a sense of camaraderie.

Creating Laughter-Filled Memories:

Explore ways to intentionally infuse humor into your friendships. This chapter provides ideas for creating laughter-filled memories, such as planning funny-themed activities or sharing amusing anecdotes. Laughter becomes a lasting thread in the fabric of your connection.

Navigating Humor Sensitivities:

While humor is powerful, it's essential to navigate sensitivities. This section offers insights into respecting boundaries and understanding diverse humor styles within friendships. Learn how to foster an environment where everyone feels comfortable and included.

Examples:

Scenario: Your friend is feeling down, and humor might lift their spirits. The role of laughter involves choosing appropriate and uplifting jokes.

Tip: Gauge your friend's mood and tailor your humor to uplift rather than unintentionally cause discomfort.

Exercise: Share a memory of a time when laughter strengthened your friendship.

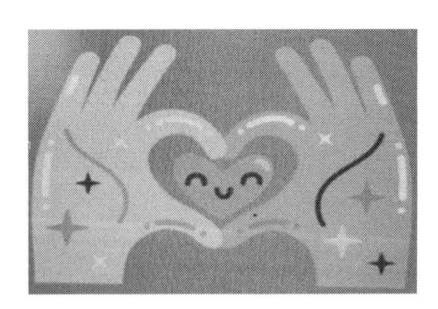

Cultivating Lifelong Learning Together

Intellectual Curiosity in Friendships:

Explore the role of intellectual curiosity in fostering dynamic and engaging friendships. This chapter discusses the value of shared interests, stimulating conversations, and the joy of learning together.

Book Clubs and Learning Circles:

Discover the benefits of joining or forming book clubs and learning circles with your friends. This section provides insights into how discussing literature, exploring new topics, or attending educational events together can deepen your connection.

Embracing Different Perspectives:

Friendships thrive on diversity of thought. This chapter encourages embracing different perspectives and engaging in respectful discussions. Learn how intellectual growth can be fueled by exposing yourself to varying viewpoints within the safe space of a friendship.

Examples:

Scenario: Your friend has a passion for a particular subject. Cultivating lifelong learning involves exploring that interest together.

Tip: Attend workshops, webinars, or events related to their passion to enhance your understanding and share the experience.

Exercise: Reflect on a time when learning something new together enriched your friendship.

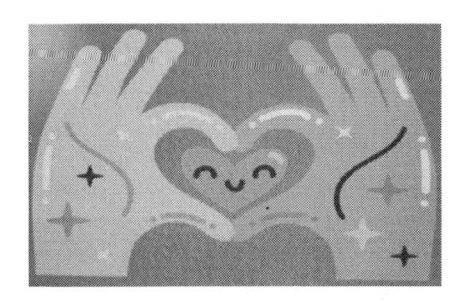

Creating Rituals and Traditions

The Significance of Rituals:

Explore how rituals and traditions contribute to the fabric of strong friendships. This chapter delves into the importance of creating shared rituals that provide a sense of continuity, belonging, and anticipation.

Personalized Friendship Rituals:

Discover the power of personalized rituals that are unique to your friendship. This section provides ideas for creating meaningful traditions, whether it's a monthly movie night, an annual trip, or a special inside joke. These rituals become anchors in your shared history.

Adapting Rituals Over Time:

Friendships evolve, and so can rituals. Learn how to adapt and modify your shared traditions to accommodate changing circumstances or preferences. This chapter provides insights into keeping the essence of rituals while allowing them to grow organically.

Example:

Scenario: Your friend moves to a different city. Adapting rituals involves finding new ways to connect and creating new traditions.

Tip: Incorporate virtual elements into existing rituals or establish new ones that suit your current situation.

Exercise: Share a memory of a cherished ritual and reflect on its significance.

Balancing Independence and Togetherness

Individual Growth Within Friendships:

Explore the delicate balance between individual growth and maintaining close friendships. This chapter emphasizes the importance of allowing each friend the space to pursue personal goals and interests while nurturing the overall connection.

Encouraging Independence:

Healthy friendships encourage individual independence. This section provides insights into supporting your friends' journeys, respecting their autonomy, and celebrating their achievements. Learn how fostering independence contributes to a robust and enduring friendship.

Reconnecting Amid Busy Lives:

Life can get busy, and priorities may shift. This chapter offers strategies for reconnecting with friends amid hectic schedules, emphasizing the quality over quantity of time spent together. Discover how intentional efforts can strengthen your bond, even amid individual pursuits.

Example:

Your friend has started a demanding new job.

Scenario:

Schedule a regular virtual coffee date to catch up on each other's lives and discuss your respective journeys.

Tip or Solution:

Acknowledge the changes in their schedule and find a rhythm that accommodates both your lives. By prioritizing intentional moments of connection, you maintain the quality of your friendship.

Gratitude and Reflection for Lasting Friendships

Reflecting on the Journey:

Take a moment to reflect on the journey of your friendships. This chapter encourages introspection and gratitude for the experiences, challenges, and growth you've shared with your friends.

Expressing Gratitude:

Discover the life-changing power of expressing gratitude within your friendships. This section provides insights into acknowledging the impact your friends have had on your life and expressing appreciation for their presence.

Building a Future Together:

Look towards the future of your friendships. This chapter explores the potential for continued growth, shared adventures, and deepening connections. Embrace the idea of building a future filled with meaningful experiences and lasting bonds.

Example:

Your friend stood by you during a challenging period.

Scenario:

Host a small gathering or send a thoughtful gift to express your gratitude.

Tip & Solution:

Take a moment to celebrate the enduring strength of your friendship. Whether through a heartfelt gesture or sincere words, expressing gratitude deepens the connection and sets the stage for continued growth.

"Sustaining Lifelong Friendships is a Continuous Journey."

The Ever-Evolving Friendship:

Understand that friendships are dynamic and ever evolving. This chapter reinforces those sustaining lifelong friendships is a continuous journey filled with opportunities for growth, adaptation, and shared joy.

Ongoing Learning and Adaptation:

Embrace the mindset of ongoing learning and adaptation within your friendships. This section emphasizes the value of staying open to new experiences, perspectives, and changes, ensuring that your connections remain vibrant and resilient.

Creating a Supportive Friendship Ecosystem:

Learn to create a supportive ecosystem within your friendship circles. This chapter discusses the importance of surrounding yourself with friends who uplift, challenge, and inspire you. By fostering a network of positive and meaningful connections, you contribute to the collective strength of your friendships.

Examples:

Scenario: Your friend embarks on a new hobby. Ongoing learning involves showing interest, participating, and sharing in their enthusiasm.

Tip: To deepen your understanding and connection, attend a workshop or event related to your hobby.

Exercise: Share a recent experience where ongoing learning enhanced your friendship.

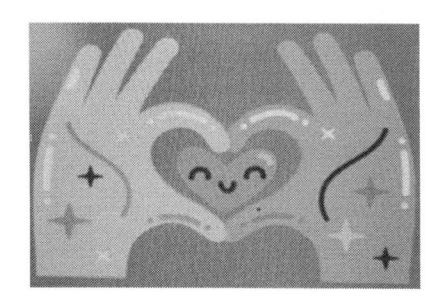

Conclusion

As you conclude this comprehensive guide to fostering lasting friendships, remember that the journey of being a great friend is ongoing. Each chapter is a steppingstone, providing insights and practical tools to enhance the quality of your connections. The experiences, examples, and exercises presented aim to empower you to navigate the complexities of friendships with grace, understanding, and authenticity.

The dynamics of friendships may evolve, but the principles of active listening, support, embracing differences, building trust, open communication, empathy, gratitude, reliability, apology, forgiveness, celebration, respecting boundaries, encouraging growth, laughter, lifelong learning, rituals, balancing independence, and reflection are timeless.

As you embark on the continuous journey of sustaining lifelong friendships, you may find joy, fulfillment, and meaningful connections that enrich your life and the lives of those you call friends. Cheers to the beautiful tapestry of friendships that weave through the fabric of our existence.

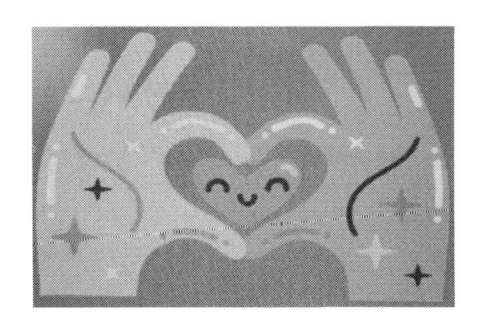

References

Covey, S. R. (1989). The 7 Habits of Highly Effective People. Free Press.

Gottman, J. M., & Silver, N. (2015). The Seven Principles for Making Marriage Work. Harmony.

Tannen, D. (1991). You Just Don't Understand: Women and Men in Conversation. HarperCollins.

Chapman, G. (1992). The Five Love Languages: How to Express Heartfelt Commitment to Your Mate. Northfield Publishing.

Carnegie, D. (1936). How to Win Friends and Influence People. Simon & Schuster.

Fredrickson, B. L. (2009). Positivity: Top-Notch Research Reveals the Upward Spiral That Will Change Your Life. Harmony.

Dweck, C. S. (2006). Mindset: The New Psychology of Success. Ballantine Books.

Barker, E. (2017). *Barking Up the Wrong Tree: The Surprising Science Behind Why Everything You Know About Success Is (Mostly) Wrong.* HarperOne.

Brown, B. (2010). *The Gifts of Imperfection: Let Go of Who You Think You're Supposed to Be and Embrace Who You Are.* Hazelden Publishing.

Ferrazzi, K. (2014). *Never Eat Alone: And Other Secrets to Success, One Relationship at a Time.* Currency.

Cain, S. (2012). *Quiet: The Power of Introverts in a World That Can't Stop Talking.* Broadway Books.

Seligman, M. E. P. (2002). *Authentic Happiness: Using the New Positive Psychology to Realize Your Potential for Lasting Fulfillment.* Free Press.

Pink, D. H. (2011). *Drive: The Surprising Truth About What Motivates Us.* Riverhead Books.

Carnegie, D. (1912). *The Dale Carnegie Course in Effective Speaking and Human Relations.* Essential Media Group.

Duckworth, A. L. (2016). *Grit: The Power of Passion and Perseverance.* Scribner.

Zak, P. J. (2015). *Trust Factor: The Science of Creating High-Performance Companies.* AMACOM.

Burns, D. D. (1989). *The Feeling Good Handbook*. Plume.

Chapman, G., & White, P. (2015). *The 5 Love Languages of Teenagers: The Secret to Loving Teens Effectively*. Northfield Publishing.

Lyubomirsky, S. (2007). *The How of Happiness: A Scientific Approach to Getting the Life You Want*. Penguin Books.

Brown, B. (2018). *Dare to Lead: Brave Work. Tough Conversations. Whole Hearts*. Random House.

Made in the USA
Columbia, SC
08 April 2024